Little Ganesha

Lord Ganesha's Birth

GODDESS Parvati has two confidants Jaya and Vijaya. They advised her to have at least one guard who obeys only her. However, Goddess Parvati dismissed this idea as she knew that all the guards and devotees of

Mahadev are **ready to obey her commands whole heartedly.**

Few days later, Goddess Parvati was tired and willing to sleep without any disturbance.

So she commanded Nandi, not to allow anyone to enter the house unless she says so. Goddess Parvati retired to her room. Only then, Mahadev visited the house for some work.

Nandi requested Mahadev not to enter the house as commanded by Goddess Parvati. But Mahadev had some important thing to do so he did not pay attention to Nandi and went inside the house. Mahadev's entry into house caused some

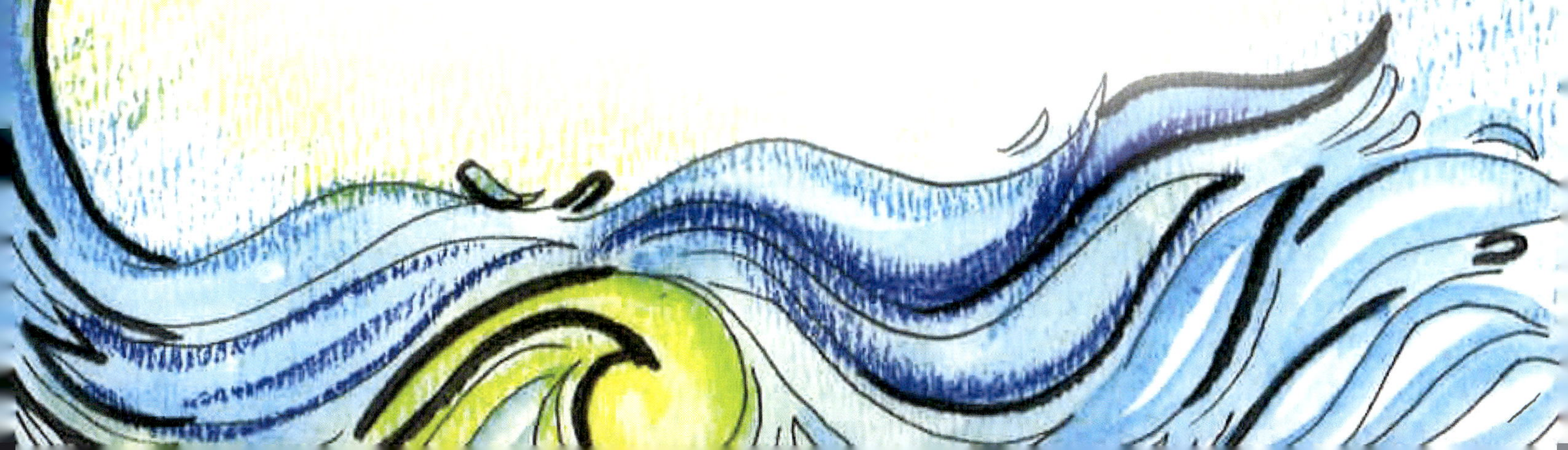

noise due to which Goddess Parvati woke up. Goddess Parvati realized that Jaya and Vijaya were right.

Jaya and Vijaya further suggested Goddess Parvati to build a kid from her body scrub and then bring it to life. Since you are cause for the Child's birth, he will obey only you. Goddess Parvati agreed and did the same. So this is how little Ganesha was born.

Story of Elephant Face

ON the very next day of Lord Ganesha's birth, Goddess Parvati required total solace in the house to do something. This time, instead of appointing any Mahadev's devotee to guard the entrance, she appointed her son.

Comfort

Few hours later, Lord Mahadev came to the house for some urgent work. But, Ganesha stopped him. Lord Mahadev tried to convince Ganesha but nothing happened. This irritated Mahadev, he left the house and sent his devotees to get the kid removed from the entrance.

To succeed in making somebody believe in something

The devotees came and tried their level best to convince Ganesha to leave the entrance for Mahadev.

However, they left disappointed. Now Mahadev Got angry. He was ordered to coercively remove the kid from entrance. This led to the war between Ganesha and Lord Mahadev's devotees. Ganesh made Mahadev's devotees bite the dust. All the Demi-Gods, Lord Brahma

Forcefully

and Lord Vishnu came to Mahadev's aid and fought on his side but nothing happened. Finally infuriated Mahadev himself led the battle and used his most powerful trident against lord Ganesha.

This time, Ganesha could not survive the attack and his head fell on the ground.

When Goddess Parvati heard about this she came running outside and cried bitterly. Seeing this, Mahadev and other Gods repented. They started thinking of something to rectify their mistake.

Finally Lord Mahadeva sent his devotee to find a head which can be placed over the neck of the deceased kid and brought back to life.

No longer living

The devotees brought an elephant's head. The head was placed over the kid and he was brought back to life. A wave of happiness crossed everyone's heart. All God and Goddesses rejoiced and gave the elephant headed Ganesha thousands of blessings.

Story of First Revered God

ONCE upon a time, All the Demi Gods started debating over whom the world should worship in the beginning of every auspicious works? When the matter converted into the heated debate, Sage Narada advised Demi-Gods to go and find a solution from Lord Mahadev.

Favourable

Lord Mahadev said that the decision of one's superiority over others would be decided by

competency and not by hollow claims. **Lord Mahadev proposed a competition** according to which all the competitors were supposed to **circumambulate**the entire universe and the one completing the

circumambulation first was supposed to be the winner. As soon as Lord Mahadev declared this competition, all the Demi Gods mounted their rides and ran. But Lord Ganesh did not move a bit.

After some time, Ganesha mounted his ride and circumambulated lord Mahadev and Goddess Parvati. When Lord Mahadev asked Ganesha the reason behind it, he said that you and Goddess Parvati are the entire universe, nothing is outside you. Others also listened to Ganesha's argument and became speechless.

With this Ganesha became the God of the beginnings.

Lesson for Lord Ganesha

GANESHA was a very naughty child. One day, as he was playing, he spotted a cat purring. He caught the cat by its tail, and decided to have some fun with it. To torment it even more, he began twisting the cat's tail until it yelled out in pain and yanked itself free of his hold. The cat then twirled around in the air, and fell with great

To make a continuous low sound

force upon the ground, injuring itself. Yowling with pain, it ran away to its home in the mountains. Ganesha rushed into his home and called out to mother Parvati to give him some food. When she came to him with the food, she was shocked to see her covered with dust, and bruised all over. She was obviously in pain.

Make a loud wailing cry

He thought to himself that his mother, being the mother of this world, is so great that nobody could have the strength to injure her in this way.

He understood that if his mother was the mother of all life on the earth, then a part of her also existed in all life. When any part of life was pained or hurt, it obviously brought great discomfort to her also. Her omnipresence in every particle of life was Divine, and the pain of the cat, which he had injured, had to be part of her pain and suffering too.

The presence of God everywhere at the same time.

Ekdant Ganesh

ONCE upon a time, a revered sage Parshuram fought a fierce battle with a King named Kartavyaveer. After defeating Kartavyaveer, Sage Parashuraam thought of receiving blessings from Lord Mahadev and came to Mount Kailash, Mahadev's abode.

However, Lord Mahadev being engaged in some other important work and had appointed Ganesha to look after the entrance. Ganesha tried to convince Parshuram to wait for a while. But the Sage infuriated being stopped by a child. Finally Parshuram started a war. Despite being lord Ganesh fought with Parshuram really well.

At the end, Parshuram took out his 'Farsa' the weapon gifted to him by Lord Mahadev. Respecting his father's gift, Ganesh did not try to stop this weapon.

The Farsa directly stuck Ganesha's tusk and broke it down.

Lord Mahadev and Goddess Parvati came running out of the house. Parshuram was regretting his action now. To amend his mistake, The sage gifted his Farsa to lord Ganesha. And this is how the Ganesha became Ekdant.

Moon's Curse

ONCE upon a time, Ganesha got angry with Lord Brahma and started scaring him assuming fierce forms. When Ganesha was doing so, Moon started laughing. This infuriated Lord Ganesha further.

Ganesha cursed the moon because of which the moon lost all his shine and glory. What is the Moon without shine and glory? He lost his visibility. Horrified, Moon went to Devlok and asked for help. However, all the Demi-Gods in Devlok knew that this is Ganesha's curse and

only he can reverse it. So all the Demi-Gods advised Moon to worship Ganesh and beg for his forgiveness.

The Moon followed the advice.

Pleased by the penance of the Moon, Lord Ganesha appeared before him.

Kind Ganesha said that his curse cannot be invalidated but it can be modified into a milder form. Lord Ganesha proclaimed that, whoever will look at the moon on the occasion of Chaturthi, he will face false charges of theft.

Till date people dont look at the moon on Ganesh Chaturthi.

A sacrament of forgivness

Riding A Rat

ONCE upon a time, Demi-God of musical art-Conch angered sage Vaamdeva. Infuriated Vaamdev cursed Conch to be a mouse. However, when Conch pleaded for mercy, the sage gave some respite to him by telling him that one day lord Ganesha will ride upon him and pacify all his sufferings.

Conch in the form of a mouse reached the hermitage of Rishi Parashar. The mouse destroyed all the gardens of hermitage and started eating everything in the kitchen of hermitage. Saddened Rishi Parashar started praying to Lord Ganesh for some relief. Impresed by his prayer Ganesha appeared.

Lord Ganesh immediately made a mystical lasso and trapped the mouse into it. Trapped by Lord Ganesh, the mouse realized his true form and the damage he had done to a sage. He started repenting. Lord Ganesh was happy as the mouse realized his mistake. He blessed him and gave him his ride.

A rope with a noose at one end

Express sincere regret

Lord Vishnu's Conch

GANESHA was very fond of Lord Vishnu's conch. One such event happened when two demons Madhu-Kaitabh emerged from Lord Vishnu's ears. The demons became very powerful after reading Brahma's Vedas. Lord Vishnu waged a war against those demons, however, Lord Vishnu appeared to be losing.

Lord Vishnu sought help from Lord Shiva. Lord Shiva in turn directed Ganesha to do something for Lord Vishnu. Obeying his father, Ganesha gave his divine powers to Lord Vishnu and made him much stronger.

Mighty Vishnu defeated Madhu Kaitabh. Lord Vishnu was very happy with Ganesha so he decided to fulfill one wish of Ganesha. Ganesha innocently asked Lord Vishnu to blow his conch. Lord Vishnu laughed at Ganesha and started blowing his conch.

End of Tripurasur

ONCE upon a time, there lived a demon named Tripurasur. Tripurasur dreamed of conquering the entire Universe. But before starting his expedition, Tripurasur worshipped lord Ganesha and took his blessings. After that mighty Tripurasur attacked Devlok. A fierce battle started between Demi-Gods and Tripurasur's forces.

A long journey for a special purpose

Demi-Gods were amazed to see the might of merely a demon.

Finally, Lord Brahma, Vishnu and Shiva, the entire holy trinity came to rescue the Demi-Gods, but all in vain. Tripurasur was so powerful this time that no one was able to match his strength.

Finally, the Gods and Goddesses took refuge in a mountain cave.

Lord Shiva was pondering over the ways to defeat Tripurasur.

Suddenly Lord Shiva realized his mistake and he along with other Gods and Demi Gods started worshipping Lord Ganesha.

Ganesha blessed all the Gods after which Lord Shiva defeated Tripurasur.

Lord Ganesh and Kaveri River

ONCE upon a time there lived a Sage - Agastya in South India. One such year entire South India faced an extreme drought. Sage Agastya was upset with the condition of his motherland and started doing extreme penance to please lord Mahadev.

Mahadev, happy with Sage Agastya's Penance, gave him an urn full of sacred water. Such was the power of the water in Urn, that it could create a source of river wherever spilled. Sage Agastya returned to his motherland. Now the sage wondered to choose a point where the water was to be spilled. Before moving ahead, The sage thought of taking a rest for a while.

A special container

But as soon as the Sage turned his back, a crow came by and spilled the water at that point and Lo! The river started flowing from that point. When Sage Agastya looked at the crow he realized that the crow was Lord Ganesha who came here to tell him that this is the most appropriate spot for the origination of the river.

A Lesson to Kuber

ONCE upon a time, the Demi-God of wealth and prosperity became too arrogant of his wealth. One day he thought of showing off his glory to all the Gods and Demi-Gods. Kuber organized a grand dinner and then went to invite everyone.

At last, he reached Kailash Mountain and invited Lord Mahadev and his family. Lord Mahadev, being omniscient, understood Kuber's intentions. He planned to taught Kuber

Knowing everything

a lesson. Mahadev called Lord Ganesha once Kuber left and make a plan.

In the evening, all the guests gathered at Kuber's house. Lord Mahadev also went there with his family. The feast started and everyone started eating the delicacies. Few hours passed, the guests started leaving, but Ganesh was still busy eating. He was still very hungry. The storage was about to empty, Kuber started trembling.

Kuber realized his folly and ran to Mahadev seeking help. Mahadev gave a 'Kalash' filled with mystic water to Kuber and asked him to go and gave it to Ganesh. Kuber did the same and indeed, Ganesha's hunger was pacified. From that day, no one saw Kuber showing off his wealth.

An act that is not sensible and may have a bad result

Calm or Quiet

Ganesha's Kheer

ONCE upon a time, Lord Ganesha thought of taking a test of devotion from his devotees. He assumed the form of a little boy and went around a village with one spoon of milk and a handful of rice. He went door to door asking to prepare milk pudding (kheer) for him with the ingredients in his hands. But, everyone laughed at him and denied entertaining his request.

Finally, outside the village, there was an impoverished old lady living in a wrecked hut. Lord Ganesha repeated his request. Old lady, being generous enough, did not deny a little boy's request and started preparing Kheer for him. Lord Ganesh was very happy with the lady's kindness. His sacred touch not only increased the quantity of Kheer to feed the entire village but he also blessed the old lady to be prosperous for once and for all.

Poor

Broken or Destroyed

An Imprint of Unbound Script

LITTLE GANESHA

First Edition : January 2025

ISBN : 978-93-92088-98-8

Publisher : Unbound Script
2/41, Ansari Road,
Daryaganj, Delhi - 110002
E-mail : books@unboundscript.com
Website : www.unboundscript.com
Phone No. : 011-35807601

Retold by Kamini Gayakwad
Illustrated by Unbound Script

Printed in India

Price: ₹199/-